Baby Jesus . . . Messiah!

as retold by Janice D. Green
illustrated by Violet V. Vandor

Honeycomb Adventures Press, LLC

Published by Honeycomb Adventures Press, LLC,
PO Box 1215, Hemingway, SC 29554.
http://honeycombadventures.com

ISBN: 978-0-9820886-2-3

Text © 2021, 2020, 2012 by Janice D. Green
Illustrations © 2021, 2020, 2012, 2011 by Violet Vandor

Baby Jesus . . . Messiah! is a re-write of the earlier full-color picture book, *The First Christmas*. It is by the same author and illustrator as the original book. This revision is more kid friendly and more accurate Biblically. A coloring book, *Baby Jesus . . . Messiah!: Color your own pictures*, is also available in this same format.

Bible references in this book are not quotations, but are paraphrases written by the author to help children understand the Biblical account of the birth of Christ Jesus.

All rights reserved. No part of this book may be reproduced or transmitted in any form or by any means, electronic or mechanical, including photo-copying, recording or by any information storage and retrieval system without the written permission of the Publisher, except where permitted by law.

Baby Jesus . . .
Messiah!

Messiah. God promised to send a Messiah, a great king, to the Jewish people and they were waiting. For hundreds of years they waited. God chose the Jewish people as his special people. When the Jews worshiped God faithfully they became a mighty nation. But they became weak when they forgot about God.

The Roman government gained control over the Jewish people when they were weak. Roman soldiers bossed them around. The Jewish people hoped Messiah would come and make the Romans leave Judea.

Messiah would soon come, quietly as a tiny baby.

How do you feel when someone bosses you around? What kind of king do you think God would send to his special people?

Zachariah and his wife Elizabeth were waiting for the Messiah. They were very old and had no children. One day while Zachariah was alone in God's Temple, God sent an angel named Gabriel to him. The angel said Elizabeth would have a son and they must name him John.

"When John grows up," Gabriel said, "he will help the people get ready for the Messiah."

Zachariah couldn't believe Gabriel. He thought it was too late for Elizabeth to have a baby. Zachariah asked Gabriel to prove his message was true.

Gabriel told Zachariah that because didn't believe God's message, he wouldn't be able to say another word until after baby John was born.

If someone told you a very old lady was going to have a baby, would you believe it? How do you think Zachariah told his wife about the angel's message without talking?

Elizabeth had a teenage cousin named Mary who was engaged to a man named Joseph. They lived in a town called Nazareth. Six months after the angel Gabriel visited Zachariah, God sent Gabriel to Nazareth with a message for Mary.

Gabriel told Mary that God would give her a baby boy and that her baby would be the Messiah! Mary asked, "How can I have a baby when I'm not yet married?" Gabriel said God's Spirit would give her the baby. Mary was happy to know she would be the mother of God's baby king.

Have you ever been chosen to do a special job? How did it make you feel?

Gabriel told Mary that her older cousin Elizabeth was also going to have a special baby. So Mary traveled a long way to visit Elizabeth.

When Elizabeth heard Mary's voice, her baby leaped inside her! Elizabeth said, "Blessed are you among women! Why have you, the mother of my Lord, blessed me with a visit? Bless you for believing the Lord's message to you."

In what ways were Mary and Elizabeth alike? How were they different? Why do you think Mary went to see Elizabeth? Who do you want to see when you have special news to share?

Mary stayed with Elizabeth for three months. That was long enough for Mary to help Elizabeth until baby John was born. The Bible doesn't say if Mary saw baby John.

While Mary stayed with Elizabeth, baby Jesus was growing inside her. By the time she returned to Nazareth, people could see that she was going to have a baby. They knew Mary was not married. Joseph did not understand. Should he still marry her?

Were you ever scolded when you hadn't done anything wrong? How did you feel? How do you think Mary felt when people looked at her and whispered mean things about her to each other?

Joseph did not know what to do.

God sent an angel to him in a dream. The angel said that Mary's baby was God's Son. The angel told Joseph not to be afraid to marry her. He said they should name the baby Jesus.

So Mary and Joseph got married knowing their son Jesus was going to be very special.

Have you ever felt like God wanted you to do something? What are some ways God might speak to us?

The Roman ruler Caesar Augustus wanted to take a census. He said everyone had to go to the city where their great-great-great-grandfathers lived hundreds of years ago. Caesar Augustus wanted to count how many people lived in the Roman Empire.

This meant that Mary and Joseph would have to travel to Bethlehem where Joseph's great-great-great-grandfathers had once lived so they could be counted. King David was one of Joseph's ancestors.

Mary grew tired. It was almost time for her baby to be born. Bethlehem was seventy miles from Nazareth. They may have had a donkey to ride. If not, they had to walk.

How do you think Mary and Joseph felt to have to walk or ride a donkey for days? Can you think of a time when you were very tired but you couldn't stop and rest?

When Mary and Joseph came to Bethlehem they saw many people rushing about looking for places to stay. They too had come to Bethlehem from other towns to be counted.

Mary and Joseph could not find a room where they could spend the night. They looked around and found a shelter where animals were kept, and did what they could to make themselves comfortable there.

Have you ever been on a trip when your father or mother couldn't find a place to stay and it was getting very late? What might you have to do if they didn't find any place to spend the night?

Jesus was born in the stable where the animals slept. Mary wrapped her baby in pieces of cloth. Baby Jesus needed a bed so Mary smoothed out a place for him in the manger. The manger may have been filled with hay for the animals to eat.

Hay is prickly, and there might have little bugs in it. But that was the best that Mary and Joseph could do for baby Jesus. The animals must have wondered why a baby was sleeping in their manger.

Have you ever visited a barn where cows and horses stay? Would you want to keep a baby in a place where cows sleep? What do you think Mary and Joseph used for their beds?

On the night baby Jesus was born, shepherds out in the fields watched their sheep like they did every night. But this night was not like other nights.

An angel appeared to them and light shown all around them. The shepherds were frightened, but the angel said, "Don't be afraid. I have good news for all people. Your Messiah is born tonight. You will find the baby lying in a manger in Bethlehem." Then more and more angels filled the sky and praised God!

How do you think you would feel if you had been one of the shepherds who heard the angel's message from God? How many times did God use an angel to give someone a message in this Bible story?

The shepherds hurried to Bethlehem and found baby Jesus lying in a manger—just like the angel said. They couldn't keep this wonder to themselves, and they hurried off to tell what happened to everyone they saw.

In those days many people thought shepherds were not important. They lived with the sheep. They smelled bad because they didn't get many chances to wash up.

But God knew shepherds were valuable. God chose shepherds to be the first people to see the Messiah and spread the good news. We wonder today how many people believed them.

How do you think the shepherds felt when they saw baby Jesus? If you had been one of the shepherds, would you want to hold Jesus, or would you think you would be too dirty to hold the baby Messiah?

Some wise men in a far away land studied the stars. One night they saw a most unusual star. Because of this special star, they knew the Jewish Messiah had been born. These wise men wanted to worship him, so they made plans and traveled hundreds of miles on camels to the land of Judea.

They went to Jerusalem, the capitol city of Judea, to ask where to find the new king, but nobody could answer their question. The priests looked through the scriptures and found that the prophet Micah said the Messiah would be born in the little town of Bethlehem.

How far have you traveled with your family? What if you had to ride on camels to get there?

The wise men hurried off toward Bethlehem to find the baby king. What Joy! When they looked in the sky they saw the same special star they had seen many months ago. This time the star went ahead of them so they could follow it, and it stopped right over the house where Mary and Joseph and Jesus were staying. Like all babies, Jesus grew while the wise men traveled so far to see him.

When the wise men saw Jesus, they bowed down and worshiped him. They gave the little king expensive gifts of gold, frankincense and myrrh.

The people wondered what baby Jesus, the Messiah, would be like when he became a man? Would he force the Romans to leave Judea? It would be thirty years before Jesus began his ministry in Judea. Many would love him, but others would hate him.

The gifts the wise men brought to Jesus were the first Christmas gifts. Whose birthday do we celebrate on Christmas? How can we give a gift to Jesus on his birthday?

Clues for the Baby Jesus puzzle

Across
2. Who were the Jewish people waiting for?
4. What did the wisemen bring to Jesus?
6. Mary's son's name
8. Who visited the shepherds?
11. Who were the first people to visit Mary and Joseph and baby Jesus?
13. The wisemen's response when they saw Jesus
15. The bed for baby Jesus
16. The place Joseph and Mary found to stay

Down
1. Transportation for the wisemen
3. Rich men who traveled a long way to see Jesus
5. The sign that told the wisemen that the Messiah was born
7. The town where Jesus was born
9. The mother of Jesus
10. The man who became Jesus' daddy
12. This animal may have provided transportation for Mary and Joseph.
14. What did shepherds take care of every day?

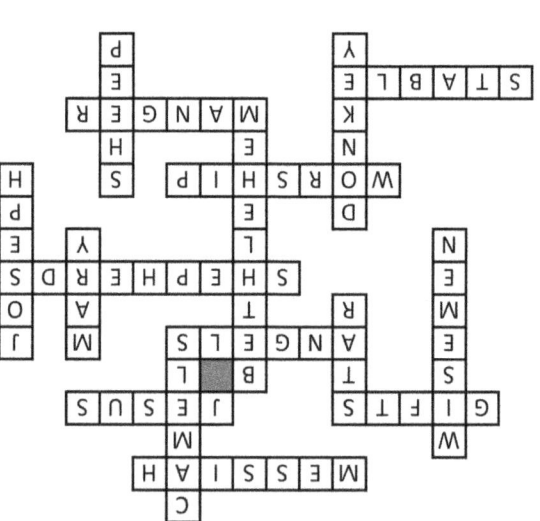

Baby Jesus

First Christmas Bible Quilt – A Family Activity

Share your excitement about the Christmas story with your children by helping them make a crayon-colored Christmas tree skirt, tablecloth, wall hanging, or quilt.

Downloadable coloring pages from this book can be traced onto pieces of quilting cotton or linen using a waterproof marker. Then you or your child can color them with crayons (Crayola^{TM} works best). Using a hot iron, press the crayon-colored pictures between paper towels to remove the wax and to set the color into the fabric. Then use your quilt blocks together with other fabric to complete your project. (For more complete instructions see www.biblequilts.com) **Download PDF file:** https://honeycombadventures.com/wp-content/uploads/2020/11/Baby-Jesus-Messiah-BQ-coloring-pages.pdf

Bible Quilts for Children's Beds

Imagine a child's bed covered by a quilt entirely made up of scenes from Bible stories. Visualize the child pointing to a picture on a square and asking to hear that Bible story again. This is the vision of BibleQuilts.com, a sister blog to Honeycomb Adventures Press, LLC.

Honeycomb Adventures Coloring Books are designed with Bible quilts in mind. *The Creation, The First Christmas*, and *Jonah: The Fearful Prophet* are "color your own" picture books with the story text on the left side and the corresponding coloring page on the right of each two-page spread. The coloring pages are also available as a download from the links found in the books and may be used for classroom teaching or for making Bible quilts.

Find Words About Jesus' Birth

ANGELS
BABYJESUS
BETHLEHEM
CAMELS
CATTLE
DONKEY
GIFTS
JOSEPH
MANGER
MARY
MESSIAH
SHEEP
SHEPHERDS
STABLE
STAR
WISEMEN
WORSHIP

```
S T A R X Y I D R S B C E H T
N A E Y R E S U W E H M P X W
S S V A M E S S I A H E A W I
G T M C N Q E S O D S N E O S
I U A X A J C K H O Q J L P E
F S A B S T N X J N W B B Q M
T T H S L W T P C A M E L S E
S R W E B E M L V Q L Y S N N
C D D F P I R N E P C A G J L
A O A J S H B E T H L E H E M
I N U L S R E G P S R L Q N V
W K G P W H H R M A N G E R I
M E T E N F L G D P X Y B N G
T Y M Q L S W O R S H I P D H
N X S R W S B A B Y J E S U S
```

About the author:

Janice D. Green retired as an elementary librarian to write books. She has published three Bible storybooks for children and made them available in three formats, color picture books, coloring books, and ebooks. Her passion is to improve Bible literacy by telling the whole story in a way that children will understand and enjoy, and that parents may learn from sharing them as well.

About the illustrator:

Violet V. Vandor has been attracted to the world of art and literature ever since she was a child. She has had more than 50 published books in Romania, Hungary, USA, Canada and the UK. In 2016-2018 she participated at international contests in Japan where she got 7 Diplomas for book illustrations, graphics, portrait and fantasy novel. Her "The Three Stone Roses" fairytale, has been performed since 2018 with big success by the Deva Art Theater's actors. In 2020 she began publishing *Pinky Elf's Realm* a free online magazine for disadvantaged children. It is published in both Hungarian and Romanian. Her website is http://violetvandor.simplesite.com/

New Releases by Honeycomb Adventures Press, LLC

The latest Honeycomb Adventures books are available in three formats to fit your situation. The full-color edition has always been the standard and continues to be available. E-books and coloring books offer a more economical way to enjoy the stories and illustrations. E-books in full color are the most economical. Coloring books contain everything that is in the full-color format, but also allows the child or an older relative or friend to color the pages and to add his or her name to the cover and title page. All three formats include a link to the downloadable PDF file that contains all the coloring pages and puzzles in the book and information on how to use the coloring pages to make a Bible quilt.

Full Color Picture Books   Full Color E-books   Coloring Books with line drawings

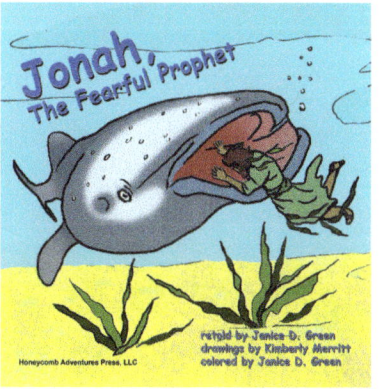  

Jonah: The Fearful Prophet shares Jonah's resistance to God's call and his second chance after being rescued from the bottom of the sea by a huge fish. This story also illustrates God's patience with Jonah and with the people of Nineveh.

The Creation gives the day-to-day Genesis account of creation and includes engaging questions for each day to encourage dialogue between the child and caregiver. Also included is a note to encourage parents and youth concerning challenges by the secular world against the creation account.

www.ingramcontent.com/pod-product-compliance
Lightning Source LLC
Chambersburg PA
CBHW061822290426
44110CB00027B/2948